PREACHING THE MYSTERY OF FAITH

The Sunday Homily

United States Conference of Catholic Bishops
Washington, DC

The document *Preaching the Mystery of Faith: The Sunday Homily* was developed by the Committee on Clergy, Consecrated Life, and Vocations, of the United States Conference of Catholic Bishops (USCCB) in collaboration with the Committees on Doctrine, Divine Worship, Evangelization and Catechesis, Cultural Diversity in the Church, Ecumenical and Interreligious Affairs, Communications, and Canonical Affairs and Church Governance. It was approved by the full body of the USCCB at its November 2012 General Meeting and has been authorized for publication by the undersigned.

Msgr. Ronny E. Jenkins, JCD
General Secretary, USCCB

CONTENTS

EXPLANATORY NOTE ON THE CAPITALIZATION OF "WORD"

Since there are multiple uses of the term "word"—such as the eternal Word and the word of God—it is important to be clear about which theological sense is being used in this text. When "Word" is capitalized, it refers to the eternal Word, the only Son begotten of the Father, who became incarnate of the Virgin Mary. When "word" is not capitalized, it refers to the broader sense of the word of God, which may include Sacred Scripture and the Tradition of the Church.

INTRODUCTION

The Church is the bearer of Christ's word to the world down through the ages until the Lord returns. This is why in her sacraments, in her authoritative teaching, in her liturgy, and in the lives of her saints, the Church proclaims the word first entrusted to the Apostles with transformative power.[1] One of the most significant ways in which the Church as the Body of Christ proclaims the dynamic word of God is through the preaching of her ordained ministers, particularly in the context of the Sunday Eucharist.[2] Preaching is nothing less than a participation in the dynamic power of the apostolic witness to the very Word that created the world, the Word that was given to the prophets and teachers of Israel, and the Word that became flesh.[3]

The Intended Audience and Purpose of This Statement

We offer this reflection on preaching to our brother priests, who, by virtue of presbyteral ordination, share in the apostolic office to preach the Gospel of Jesus Christ,[4] as well as to our deacons, who may preach the homily in accord with the provisions of canon law as ministers of the word.[5] We also address those who are responsible for the formation and training of future priests and deacons as well as those who conduct continuing education programs for clergy, inviting them all to take to heart this reflection on the ministry

---

1   See *Catechism of the Catholic Church* (CCC), nos. 2-3.
2   See *Code of Canon Law* (CIC), c. 767 §§1-2; *Code of Canons of the Eastern Churches* (CCEO), c. 614 §§1-2.
3   See *Dei Verbum* (*Dogmatic Constitution on Divine Revelation*), no. 8: "Thus, the apostolic preaching, which is expressed in a special way in the inspired books, was to be preserved in a continuous line of succession until the end of time. . . . What was handed on by the apostles comprises everything that serves to make the People of God live their lives in holiness and increase their faith. In this way the Church, in her doctrine, life and worship, perpetuates and transmits to every generation all that she herself is, all that she believes." (Citations from Vatican II documents are taken from *Vatican Council II: Volume 1: The Conciliar and Post-Conciliar Documents*, ed. Austin Flannery [Northport, NY: Costello Publishing Company, 1996].)
4   See *Presbyterorum Ordinis* (*Decree on the Life and Ministry of Priests*), II, 4.
5   See *National Directory for the Formation, Ministry, and Life of Permanent Deacons in the United States* (Washington, DC: United States Conference of Catholic Bishops [USCCB], 2005), no. 35, p. 19; CIC, c. 764.

of preaching in the context of the Sunday Eucharist in the special circumstances and needs of our time.

We recognize that qualified lay persons may be authorized to preach in churches and oratories, and we are grateful for the ways in which they enrich the Church through their proclamation of God's word.[6] We hope what is said here might also be useful for all those who cooperate with the bishop and his presbyters in the ministry of the divine word.[7] However, our focus in this statement is on preaching the Sunday homily, which is reserved to the ordained minister and which offers an ordinary and urgent opportunity for the Church to bring the gospel message to her people. The vast majority of such preaching takes place in the context of the parish, but we are aware that the Church gathers in various settings to celebrate the Lord's Day—in hospital chapels, in prisons, in campus ministry settings, and even on the battlefield.

We are prompted to offer this reflection by Pope Benedict XVI's call for a renewal of the preaching ministry in the wake of the October 2008 Twelfth Ordinary General Assembly of the Synod of Bishops on "The Word of God in the Life and Ministry of the Church." In the post-synodal apostolic exhortation *Verbum Domini*, the Holy Father states that the word of God is "a wellspring of constant renewal" in the Church and a power that "will be ever more fully at the heart of every ecclesial activity."[8] Given the importance of the word of God, the Holy Father repeated his statement from the post-synodal apostolic exhortation *Sacramentum Caritatis* that "the quality of homilies needs to be improved."[9] In this earlier document, the Holy Father had also warned that the catechetical aim of the homily should not be forgotten.[10]

We are also aware that in survey after survey over the past years, the People of God have called for more powerful and inspiring preaching. A steady diet of tepid or poorly prepared homilies is often cited as a cause for discouragement on the part of laity and even leading some to turn away from the Church.

---

6   See CIC, c. 766; USCCB Complementary Norm to c. 766 (*www.usccb.org/beliefs-and-teachings/what-we-believe/canon-law/complementary-norms/canon-766-lay-preaching.cfm*); CCEO, cc. 608, 610 §4.
7   See CIC, c. 759; CCEO, c. 608.
8   Pope Benedict XVI, post-synodal apostolic exhortation *Verbum Domini* (*The Word of the Lord*), no. 1.
9   *Verbum Domini*, no. 59.
10   See Pope Benedict XVI, post-synodal apostolic exhortation *Sacramentum Caritatis* (*The Sacrament of Charity*), no. 46.

Preaching the Sunday Homily and the Current Pastoral Context of the Church in the United States

Thirty years ago, the former Committee on Priestly Life and Ministry issued the document *Fulfilled in Your Hearing: The Homily in the Sunday Assembly*.[11] This text has proven very helpful in the life and mission of the Church, especially in the formation of preachers. However, new circumstances within the Church at this historical moment call for us to build on this previous document and to reflect anew on the ministry of preaching.

In the years since *Fulfilled in Your Hearing* was published, the Church, under the leadership of Blessed John Paul II and Pope Benedict XVI, has emphasized the need to engage in a "New Evangelization," a call for a renewal of the Church first articulated by Pope Paul VI in his apostolic exhortation *Evangelii Nuntiandi*.[12] In order for the Church to fulfill her mission "to the nations," she must continually renew herself in her own members. In our day many Catholics have drifted away from active participation in the Church and are in need themselves of hearing again the Gospel of Jesus Christ and of recommitting themselves to discipleship.

At its heart, the New Evangelization is the re-proposing of the encounter with the Risen Lord, his Gospel, and his Church to those who no longer find the Church's message engaging. Pope Benedict XVI has presented the New Evangelization as the focus, mission, and ministry of the Church going into the future: "Recovering the centrality of the divine word in the Christian life leads us to appreciate anew the deepest meaning of the forceful appeal of Pope John Paul II: to pursue the *missio ad gentes* and vigorously to embark upon the new evangelization, especially in those nations where the Gospel has been forgotten or meets with indifference as a result of widespread secularism."[13] In order to awaken this hunger and thirst for the word of God in our time, we need to renew our preaching with lively faith, firm conviction, and joyful witness.

In announcing 2012-13 as a "Year of Faith," Pope Benedict XVI declared: "What the world is in particular need of today is the credible witness of

---

11   USCCB, *Fulfilled in Your Hearing: The Homily in the Sunday Assembly* (Washington DC: USCCB, 1982).
12   Pope Paul VI, *Evangelii Nuntiandi* (*On Evangelization in the Modern World*); Pope John Paul II, *Redemptoris Missio* (*On the Permanent Validity of the Church's Missionary Mandate*), no. 3.
13   *Verbum Domini*, no. 122.

people enlightened in mind and heart by the word of the Lord, and capable of opening the hearts and minds of many to the desire for God and for true life, life without end."[14] More than ever, therefore, an increasingly important objective of the Sunday homily in our day is to stir the hearts of our people, to deepen their knowledge of the faith, and to renew their living the faith in the world and participation in the Church and her sacraments.

Indeed, the Church in the United States faces a number of challenges that compel us to call for a renewed consideration of the Church's mission to proclaim God's word. We know, for example, that through immigration the Catholic population is increasingly diverse in its cultural and ethnic makeup, and this diversity is found in many parishes, particularly those in urban areas. This diversity is a great blessing for our Church and our country, but it also raises new challenges for those who preach in such settings.

Likewise, recent studies have shown that many Catholics, for a variety of reasons, seem either indifferent to or disaffected with the Church and her teaching:

- We know that the general social context in the United States has a strong emphasis on the individual and individual choice, which often eclipses the sense of community or of the common good that is essential to Christian life.
- Sadly, too, we must confess that the sexual abuse crisis has wounded the Church, and this scandal has led some Catholics to lose heart and leave the Church.
- While our society is dynamic and our country blessed with many resources and opportunities, there are sharp polarities in our political life today and, on the part of many, an undertow of uncertainty about our future.
- Pope Benedict XVI has frequently lamented the spirit of relativism that dominates the perspectives of many in our modern Western world, where absolute truth or enduring values are considered illusory—making the preaching of the eternal truth of the Gospel all the more difficult.
- While many people in the United States still enjoy the bounty of this land, there is also a feverish sense of consumerism and a focus on material satisfaction to the detriment of spiritual values.

---

14   Pope Benedict XVI, *Porta Fidei* (*www.vatican.va/holy_father/benedict_xvi/motu_proprio/documents/ hf_ben-xvi_motu-proprio_20111011_porta-fidei_en.html*), no. 15.

- At the same time, the gap between rich and poor seems to be growing in our society, and a severe economic crisis takes a terrible toll.
- Although there have been advances made to overcome the sin of racism, we still have attitudes of prejudice that violate the dignity of the human person.
- While many young adults are idealistic and search out ways to be of service to society, there is also grave concern that the participation of young adults in the life of the Church has declined in a significant way.

We also recognize that many Catholics, even those who are devoted to the life of the Church and hunger for a deeper spirituality, seem to be uninformed about the Church's teaching and are in need of a stronger catechesis. At a time when living an authentic Christian life leads to complex challenges, people need to be nourished all the more by the truth and guidance of their Catholic faith. Aware of this present social context and realizing the need for a deeper evangelization among our Catholic population, with renewed vigor the Church's preachers must inspire and instruct the faithful in the beauty and truth of Catholic Tradition and practice.

We believe that the current circumstances of our world and the call for a fresh spirit of evangelization provide a connection between *Fulfilled in Your Hearing* and the present document. The former gave particular attention to the dynamics of composing an effective Sunday homily—practical wisdom that remains valid. Yet the homilist of today must realize that he is addressing a congregation that is more culturally diverse than previously, one that is profoundly affected by the surrounding secular agenda and, in many instances, inadequately catechized. The Church's rich theological, doctrinal, and catechetical tradition must therefore properly inform the preaching task in its liturgical setting, for Jesus Christ must be proclaimed in a new way and with new urgency, and the Sunday liturgy remains the basic setting in which most adult Catholics encounter Christ and their Catholic faith. Therefore this statement will give special attention to the biblical and theological foundations for effective liturgical preaching and will consider the proper connection between the Sunday homily and the Church's liturgy and catechesis.

We intend that this theological and pastoral reflection on the Sunday homily will be followed by the publication of practical resources that will help renew the preaching ministry of the Church, so urgent at this time.

The Approach of This Statement

We will begin our reflection on the Sunday homily by turning first to its theological and biblical foundations. As *Fulfilled in Your Hearing* turned for inspiration to the dramatic scene of Jesus' inaugural preaching in the Gospel of Luke, so too will we turn to Luke's Gospel for our reflection on the preaching ministry of Jesus, not only in the beginning of Jesus' ministry but in the beautiful account of the disciples on the way to Emmaus that leads the Gospel to its conclusion. Throughout the text we will also consider other rich biblical examples that illustrate the full scope of our preaching ministry.

We will then concentrate on the intrinsic interconnection between the Scriptures, the homily and its liturgical context, and the Church's teaching and catechesis. Here the particular pastoral needs of our time that have prompted the call for a renewed evangelization are an important context.

Finally, we conclude our reflection with a consideration of the spirituality of the homilist. We will consider the necessary qualities of an effective preacher as well as the demands placed upon one who is called to the sacred task of interpreting the Scriptures and preaching the Sunday homily. What might we do as ministers of the word to develop ourselves personally to improve the quality of preaching in our day?

I. The Biblical Foundations for the Church's Preaching Ministry

Jesus, the Word of God Incarnate, and the Preaching Mission of the Apostles

The ultimate foundation for the Church's preaching ministry reaches to the opening chapters of Genesis where we learn that God, before the beginning of time, reveals himself through his creative and powerful Word. As Pope Benedict XVI notes in *Verbum Domini*, "The novelty of biblical revelation consists in the fact that God becomes known through the dialogue which he desires to have with us."[15] Indeed our Trinitarian faith professes a God who in his very essence of infinite love is relational and self-communicating. The Father, from all eternity, is never silent. He, in the love of the Holy Spirit, eternally speaks his word, who is his co-equal Son.

In the love of the Holy Spirit, the Father creates everything through his Son. Thus the Scriptures present the Word of God as all-powerful, creating the universe that teems with life and beauty and, with human beings as the pinnacle of material creation, shapes them male and female in his own image and likeness. Impelled by love, God, through his Word, gives reality and meaning to all of creation. The poetic words of the prophet Isaiah capture this fundamental biblical conviction: "Just as from the heavens the rain and snow come down and do not return there till they have watered the earth, making it fertile and fruitful, giving seed to the one who sows . . . so shall my

---

15   *Verbum Domini*, no. 6.

word be that goes forth from my mouth; my word shall not return to me void, but shall do my will, achieving the end for which I sent it" (Is 55:10-11).[16]

As the Holy Father notes in *Verbum Domini*, the New Testament parallel to the reflection on God's creative Word in Genesis is found in the Prologue of John's Gospel. "In reality, the Word of God, through whom 'all things were made' (Jn 1:3) and who 'became flesh' (Jn 1:14), is the same Word who is 'in the beginning' (Jn 1:1)."[17] In the light of this, Christian faith professes that the Word through whom the Father created the universe and guides the course of human history is the same Word who became flesh and dwelt among us. It is Jesus Christ, the Word Incarnate, who saves the world through his Death and Resurrection and gives new life to the world by the outpouring of his Holy Spirit. As Pope Benedict XVI relates in *Verbum Domini*, "Now the word is not simply audible; not only does it have a *voice*, now the word has a *face*, one which we can see: that of Jesus of Nazareth."[18]

Therefore the Gospels consistently portray the divine power of Jesus' words. At the tomb of his friend, "he cried out in a loud voice, 'Lazarus, come out!' The dead man came out . . . " (Jn 11:43-44). Kneeling next to a young child who had died, he said, "'Little girl, I say to you, arise!' The girl, a child of twelve, arose immediately and walked around" (Mk 5:41-42). With his frightened disciples in a boat during a storm on the Sea of Galilee, he "rebuked the wind, and said to the sea, 'Quiet! Be still!' The wind ceased and there was great calm" (Mk 4:39). Precisely because he is the Divine Word, what Jesus speaks comes to be.

This mission of proclaiming the Word was entrusted to the Apostles in the wake of the Resurrection. Through the gift of the Spirit lavished on the Church at Pentecost, the Apostles immediately began to proclaim the Gospel to the crowds present in Jerusalem (Acts 2:1-4). That dynamic and urgent mission of proclamation would continue as the Spirit impelled the Apostles and other missionaries to carry the message of the Risen Christ to the world.

Even so, there is a difference in kind between the preaching of Jesus and the preaching of the Apostles. Jesus, though bearing testimony to the Father, also bears testimony to himself.[19] The Apostles, for their part, bear testimony

---

16   Scripture translations are from the *Lectionary for Mass for Use in the Dioceses of the United States of America, second typical edition* © 2001, 1998, 1997, 1986, 1970 Confraternity of Christian Doctrine, Inc., Washington, DC; otherwise, from the *New American Bible, revised edition* (NABRE).
17   *Verbum Domini*, no. 6.
18   *Verbum Domini*, no. 12.
19   See Lk 4:21; Jn 3:11; 5:31-47; 8:14-18; 10:25; 15:26; 1 Tm 6:13; 1 Jn 5:7-8.

not to themselves but to Jesus. He indeed becomes the principal content of their preaching. Beginning with the preaching ascribed to Peter in the Acts of the Apostles, the texts of the Old Testament are referred to Jesus, to his Death and Resurrection. Ultimately the Lord's Paschal Mystery becomes the basis of all preaching.

That this kind of preaching begins on Pentecost is no accident. Christian preaching derives from the Risen Lord and finds its voice and force through the gift of the Holy Spirit. As Paul himself affirmed, "No one can say, 'Jesus is Lord,' except by the Holy Spirit" (1 Cor 12:3). And further, "God sent the Spirit of his Son into our hearts, crying out, 'Abba, Father!'" (Gal 4:6). This defines the preacher's task: enabling the whole community and each individual believer to draw on the power of the Holy Spirit and to say with one's whole being, "Jesus is Lord," and to cry out to God, "Abba, Father!" To preach Christ is ultimately to preach "the mystery of God," to preach the one "in whom are hidden all the treasures of wisdom and knowledge" (Col 2:2-3).

The Mission of Jesus as Preacher of the Word

We can think of ourselves as apprentices to Jesus the Master and so draw inspiration and learning about preaching from the example of Jesus himself as presented in the Gospels. Using the technique of *lectio divina*, which Pope Benedict XVI has recommended to all believers, we are able to absorb more deeply the breathtaking beauty and power of the Scriptures.[20] This venerable method of approaching the Scriptures, the pope observes, begins with a prayerful reading of the biblical text, then a meditation on its message, followed by a prayerful response on our part concerning what the Lord may ask of us through this biblical passage, and finally, contemplation of what conversion of heart and mind will be necessary to bring the message of the word to action in our lives and those of others. It is that movement from prayerful attentiveness to the word to reflection on its meaning and to proclamation of the message in speech and action that undergirds the preaching ministry itself and provides the logic of this statement.

---

20   See *Verbum Domini*, nos. 86-87.

The Kingdom of God as the Keynote of Jesus' Preaching Mission

The key motif of Jesus' preaching in the Synoptic Gospels is his announcement of the coming Reign of God: "After John had been arrested, Jesus came to Galilee proclaiming the gospel of God: 'This is the time of fulfillment. The kingdom of God is at hand. Repent, and believe in the gospel'" (Mk 1:14-15). Jesus' words are a dramatic summons to attention and response. The moment that the people of Israel had longed for was about to appear. Jesus wanted to wake his people from their spiritual slumber to hear the Good News of God's deliverance.

What is now at hand is the "Kingdom" or "Reign" of God. The Bible firmly proclaims that God alone is the Sovereign of Israel; human monarchs can only serve on God's behalf. The repeated failures of some of Israel's kings to administer God's justice, particularly to the poor and vulnerable, and the spiritual corruption of its political structures through the centuries led to a longing that God himself would ultimately come to liberate Israel at the end of the age and to transform her into a holy people, a people who would know the fullness of peace and justice, the fruits of the Covenant. God's "Reign" or "Kingdom" was a way of speaking of God's own redeeming presence and therefore would mean healing and forgiveness, true justice and lasting peace. Thus Jesus makes the Kingdom of God the keynote of his mission and teaches his disciples to pray to the Father: "Thy Kingdom come" (Mt 6:10).

Jesus himself is the embodiment of the Kingdom of God. Through his words of truth and forgiveness and his healing actions during his earthly ministry, Jesus already anticipated the fullness of the Kingdom of God that would be realized at the end of time. Origen of Alexandria called Jesus himself the *autobasilea*, the "Kingdom in person."[21] Jesus, the Incarnate Son of God, is the realization of the deepest hopes of Israel: the perfection of the covenant, the temple par excellence, the supreme prophetic Word, and the meeting of the faithful God and obedient Israel. It is this dramatic Good News that Jesus announces at the very beginning of his mission in Galilee.

All effective homilies have this sense of urgency and freshness, revealing the startling beauty and promise of the Kingdom of God and of Jesus who

---

21 In Origen's commentary on the Gospel of Matthew, *Patrologia Graeca* XIII (1862), p. 1197. See also the words of St. Ambrose, "Where Christ is, there is his kingdom," quoted in the CCC, no. 1025.

embodies it and brings it to reality through his Death and Resurrection. The message of the Gospel is truly a matter of "life and death" for us; there is nothing routine or trivial about it. If a homilist conveys merely some example of proverbial wisdom or good manners, or only some insight gained from his personal experience, he may have spoken accurately and even helpfully, but he has not yet spoken the Gospel, which ultimately must focus on the person of Jesus and the dynamic power of his mission to the world.

Since the Kingdom of God is at hand, the only proper response is a radical change of heart: "Repent, and believe in the gospel" (Mk 1:15). The Greek word that lies behind "repent" here is *metanoiete*, which literally means a "change of mind" or "change of perspective." Jesus invites his first hearers to turn from sin, to change their attitude, their entire manner of living, and to now see reality in the light of the Gospel, the Good News of God. This is why every effective homily is a summons to conversion. The announcement of the Kingdom through the words and examples of the homily, if it is clear and compelling, inevitably leads the hearer to a desire to be changed.

The need for repentance does not mean that homilies should simply berate the people for their failures. Such an approach is not usually effective, for concentrating on our sinfulness, unaccompanied by the assurance of grace, usually produces either resentment or discouragement. Preaching the Gospel entails challenge but also encouragement, consolation, support, and compassion. For this reason many teachers of homiletics warn, quite legitimately, against "moralizing" homilies, which harp excessively or exclusively on sin and its dangers. But when the offer of grace is also clear and presented with pastoral sensitivity, the recipient of that grace wants to change and wants to know what the new life in Christ looks like concretely. We think of the people's heartfelt response to Peter after his Pentecost discourse: "What are we to do, my brothers?" (Acts 2:37).

At the same time, our responsibility toward our brothers and sisters in Christ includes the need for "fraternal correction" done in a spirit of charity and truth. As Pope Benedict XVI noted in his Lenten reflections for 2012, "We must not remain silent before evil. I am thinking of all those Christians who, out of human regard or purely personal convenience, adapt to the prevailing mentality, rather than warning their brothers and sisters against ways of thinking and acting that are contrary to the truth and that do not follow the path of goodness. Christian admonishment, for its part, is never motivated by a spirit of accusation or recrimination."[22]

The command that immediately follows "repent" is "believe the good news." The Greek term that translates as "believe" is *pisteuete*, and this word carries the sense of trust or confidence. Belief involves accepting Jesus and his teachings as Good News, which is handed on in the living tradition of the Church. Faith is a matter of the mind and the heart and the will. The unrepentant person trusts in himself or in some worldly value, but the converted person has the courage to trust in Christ, which is to say, to place one's entire life in Christ's hands, a radical healing and renewal of the whole person. A good homily is an occasion to find healing precisely through confidence in Christ Jesus. This is why it is crucial that the homilist be a man of faith, capable of making the reality of his faith visible and radiant. Catholic laity want their homilist to be passionate and excited about what he is preaching, and to deliver homilies that are heartfelt and drawn from the depths of his own faith and commitment.

Jesus as Prophet and Teacher in the Gospel of Luke

To draw further instruction about homiletic preaching from the Scriptures themselves, we turn first to the famous scene in the Gospel of Luke where Jesus preaches in his hometown synagogue of Nazareth (Lk 4:14-30). It can also highlight, in the spirit of *lectio divina*, this statement's emphasis on the proper connection between the Sunday homily, the Eucharist, and the context of the Church's catechesis needed for today. In addition to this passage we will also turn to Luke's account of the Risen Jesus' appearance to the disciples on the road to Emmaus (Lk 24:13-35).

As is the case with each of the Gospels, Luke presents Jesus as a dynamic proclaimer of the word of God, driven by the power of the Spirit (Lk 4:14; 4:43-45). Jesus' role as God's definitive prophet is a particular emphasis of Luke's portrayal. This is clear in the opening scene of Jesus' public ministry in the synagogue of Nazareth (Lk 4:16-30), which serves as a kind of overture or keynote of the entire mission of Jesus. Preaching on a Sabbath (which Luke

---

22   Message of His Holiness Pope Benedict XVI for Lent 2012, November 3, 2011 (*www.vatican.va/ holy_father/benedict_xvi/messages/lent/documents/hf_ben-xvi_mes_20111103_lent-2012_en.html*).

notes was "according to his custom"), Jesus chooses the passage from Isaiah 61, which proclaims God's liberating justice: "The Spirit of the Lord is upon me, because he has anointed me to bring glad tidings to the poor. He has sent me to proclaim liberty to captives and recovery of sight to the blind, and to let the oppressed go free, and to proclaim a year acceptable to the Lord." As the entire congregation hangs on his words, Jesus rolls up the scroll, hands it back to the attendant, and dramatically proclaims: "Today this scripture passage is fulfilled in your hearing."

So here at the outset of Luke's Gospel, we can find in the inaugural prophetic preaching of Jesus a connection to the Church's ongoing mission, including the particular circumstances of our own day and the need for evangelization. Proclaiming the message of the Kingdom preached by and embodied in Jesus' person and mission is intrinsically linked to the Church's mission of justice, a constant and powerful message, amplified in a strong way in the teaching of recent popes. A straight line can be drawn from the call for justice on behalf of those who are vulnerable in the Old Testament ("the widow, the orphan, and the stranger") to the fulfillment of that mission of compassion and justice in the ministry of Jesus (and taught in the ongoing Magisterium of the Church). The Church's urgent call for respect for human life, particularly for those who are most vulnerable, the call for justice for the poor and the migrant, the condemnation of oppression and violations of human and religious freedom, and the rejection of violence as an ordinary means of solving conflicts are some of the controversial issues that need to be part of the Church's catechesis and to find their way in an appropriate manner into the Church's liturgical preaching.[23]

Luke's beautiful account of the Risen Christ's encounter with two of his followers on the road to Emmaus (24:13-35) also provides powerful insights into the ministry of liturgical preaching. Two discouraged disciples leave Jerusalem after the events of Good Friday, their hopes that Jesus was the promised redeemer of Israel having apparently been proven to be in vain. The entire momentum of the Gospel of Luke leans toward Jerusalem, the city of the Passion and Death of Jesus, the city of the Resurrection and the sending of the Spirit. Yet these two disappointed and confused disciples are heading *away* from Jerusalem. At the same time, we know that they cannot forget Jesus, who had captured their hearts and fired their hopes. On their way they discuss

---

23   See CIC, c. 768 §2; CCEO, c. 616 §2.

13

all that had happened to Jesus, "a prophet mighty in deed and word before God and all the people" (Lk 24:19). They are, accordingly, evocative of all the followers of Jesus throughout the centuries to the present day: seeking the Lord, fascinated by him, but at times bewildered and even disillusioned and apt to walk the wrong path.

We can draw several important lessons for homiletic preaching from this rich Gospel account.

1. The Paschal Mystery Informs Human Experience

Jesus comes to join the two disciples, though at first they are prevented from recognizing him. To provoke a response, Jesus asks them what they were discussing. One of them, Cleopas, answers, "The things that have taken place [in regard to Jesus of Nazareth]." When pressed, "What sort of things?" (Lk 24:19), Cleopas offers a succinct summary of the major events of Jesus' life and ministry: he was a prophet mighty in word and deed; he was handed over by the chief priests and leaders; he was crucified and put to death; there was even a report that he had risen from the dead. In short, these disciples have the basic facts but they do not yet understand their profound meaning.

And this is why Jesus says to them, "Oh, how foolish you are! How slow of heart to believe all that the prophets spoke! Was it not necessary that the Christ should suffer these things and enter into his glory?" (Lk 24:25). What would enable them to see Jesus in full, the indispensible key to interpreting him, was nothing other than the self-emptying love of the Messiah revealed in his Death and Resurrection. Everything that Christ taught and all of his actions were conditioned by this outpouring of life on behalf of others, the heart of the Paschal Mystery.

It is in this vein that Jesus then turns his disciples' attention to the Scriptures, and "beginning with Moses and all the prophets, he interpreted to them what referred to him in all the scriptures" (Lk 24:23). The sacred writings of the Old Testament, which these disciples knew well, now took on a new resonance as they were placed in relation to Jesus and his life-giving Death and Resurrection. A fundamental conviction of the New Testament is that

14

the hopes and longings of the Old Testament were not in vain but find their fulfillment in the person and mission of Jesus.[24]

This familiar and deceptively simple passage carries enormous implications for preaching in the setting of the Sunday Eucharist. First, the homilist is speaking to people who are, at least to some degree, searching for Jesus Christ and the meaning that the Gospel can give to their lives. This is what ultimately draws them to the Eucharist, no matter how fragile their faith and understanding might be. The homilist, therefore, addresses disciples who—like their spiritual ancestors on the road to Emmaus—may be tending, in varying degrees, in the wrong direction, confused and unsure. Indeed, the *Kyrie, eleison*, the traditional plea for Christ's mercy at the opening of the Eucharist, takes for granted precisely this fact that we are sinners who have lost our way. Those who hear a homily may be aware of the basic facts about Jesus, but they might grasp only vaguely or inadequately what draws that data into a pattern of profound and ultimate meaning for human life.

Homilies are inspirational when they touch the deepest levels of the human heart and address the real questions of human experience. Pope Benedict XVI, in his encyclical *Spe Salvi*, spoke of people having "little hopes" and the "great hope." "Little hopes" are those ordinary experiences of joy and satisfaction we often experience: the love of family and friends, the anticipation of a vacation or a family celebration, the satisfaction of work well done, the blessing of good health, and so on. But underneath these smaller hopes must pulsate a deeper "great hope" that ultimately gives meaning to all of our experience: the hope for life beyond death, the thirst for ultimate truth, goodness, beauty, and peace, the hope for communion with God himself. As the pope expresses it, "Let us say once again: we need the greater and lesser hopes that keep us going day by day. But these are not enough without the great hope, which must surpass everything else. This great hope can only be God, who encompasses the whole of reality and who can bestow upon us what we, by ourselves, cannot attain."[25]

Every homily, because it is an intrinsic part of the Sunday Eucharist, must therefore be about the dying and rising of Jesus Christ and his sacrificial passage through suffering to new and eternal life for us. By means of that pattern, the People of God can understand their own lives properly and be able to

---

24   See The Pontifical Biblical Commission, *The Jewish People and Their Sacred Scriptures in the Christian Bible* (TJPSS) (Libreria Editrice Vaticana, 2002), nos. 19-21.

25   Pope Benedict XVI, *Spe Salvi* (*On Christian Hope*), nos. 30-31.

see their own experience in the light of the Death and Resurrection of Jesus. In light of the encounter on the road to Emmaus, an essential element of all good preaching is evident: reflecting on our personal and collective experience in the light of the Paschal Mystery.

2. The Mutual Illumination of the Old and New Testaments

Jesus often built his teaching about the Paschal Mystery on the firm foundation of the Old Testament. His practice affirms for us that the preaching of the Sunday homily should typically involve the bringing together, in mutual illumination, of the Old Testament and the New Testament.[26] Indeed, the Sunday readings in lectionaries revised after the Second Vatican Council were chosen to demonstrate this very connection.

A Sunday Old Testament reading, for example, both speaks of God's actions among his Chosen People, the Jews, and points toward Christ, the Messiah, whose teaching and example are found in the day's Gospel passage. The Responsorial Psalm, along with its antiphon, often echoes underlying motifs found in the readings and gives voice to the faith of those who hear God's word. The homiletic practice of both the Latin Rite and the Eastern Churches has always shown how the Old and New Testaments blend together into the single voice of God speaking to his people in two important ways. First, the New Testament recognizes the authority of the Old Testament as revealed by God, who thereby shows us his plan for salvation. Second, the New Testament appropriates the writings of the Old Testament by developing them in the light of Jesus Christ.[27] It is in connection with this latter step that St. Augustine formulated his now-famous dictum: "In the old the new lies hidden; in the new the old comes to light."[28]

For the Christian, Jesus' fulfillment of the Old Testament attributes the utmost importance to the truth of the Jewish Scriptures.[29] Of course, the supreme reader of the Old Testament is Christ himself, who applied to his

---

26 For a complete exposition on the relationship of the Old and New Testaments relative to preaching, see the Vatican Commission for Religious Relations with Jews, "Notes on the Correct Way to Present Jews and Judaism" (1985), as well as its "Guidelines and Suggestions for Implementing the Conciliar Declaration Nostra Aetate," no. 4 (1974), and the USCCB's "God's Mercy Endures Forever: Guidelines on the Presentation of Jews and Judaism in Catholic Preaching" (1988).
27 See TJPSS, 14.
28 Quaestiones in Heptateuchum, no. 2, 73: PL 34, 623.
29 See TJPSS, nos. 20-21.

own life, Death, and Resurrection all that the Scriptures had promised (Lk 24:27).[30] It is through this rich relationship between the Old and the New Testaments, in all of their various interrelated images and types, that the homilist is able to proclaim to the faithful the one supreme mystery of faith that is Jesus Christ.

3. The Sunday Homily as Integral to the Eucharist

The Gospels more than once portray Jesus preaching in the context of the Sabbath synagogue service, such as in Luke's opening scene of Jesus' ministry. They also present Jesus offering profound reflections to his disciples in the context of the last Passover meal celebrated on the eve of his Death (see Jn 13-17). Luke concludes the Emmaus narrative with Jesus staying with his disciples to share a meal with them and, in so doing, revealing to them his presence. As the travelers come near the town to which they are going, they press their mysterious friend to stay with them. He sits down with them, gives thanks, and breaks bread, at which point they recognize him and he vanishes from their sight. It is then that they admit to one another that their hearts had been "burning within" them as Jesus opened the meaning of the Scriptures for them (Lk 24:32). The Emmaus account illuminates the interpenetration of the two dimensions of the Eucharistic liturgy. Jesus' explanation of the Scriptures (the Liturgy of the Word) leads to an intense experience of communion with the Risen Christ (the Liturgy of the Eucharist), and the very vividness of the latter brings about a deeper appreciation of the former ("Were not our hearts burning within us?").

One of the most important teachings of Vatican II in regard to preaching is the insistence that the homily is an integral part of the Eucharist itself.[31] As part of the entire liturgical act, the homily is meant to set hearts on fire with praise and thanksgiving. It is to be a feature of the intense and privileged encounter with Jesus Christ that takes place in the liturgy. One might even say that the homilist connects the two parts of the Eucharistic liturgy as he looks back at the Scripture readings and looks forward to the sacrificial meal. This is why it is preferable that the celebrant of the Eucharistic liturgy also be the homilist.[32] In addition, this very integration of the homily into

---

30 See TJPSS, no. 43.
31 See *Sacrosanctum Concilium* (*Constitution on the Sacred Liturgy*), no. 52.
32 See *The General Instruction of the Roman Missal* (GIRM), no. 66.

the texture of the liturgy warrants the use of the Lectionary readings as the basis for the homily.[33] A proper focus on the Lectionary readings as the prime source of the homily does not in any way preclude the homilist's illustrating the implications of the biblical message also through reference to the orations of the particular Sunday liturgy, to elements of the Creed, to the Eucharistic Prayer, or to Church teaching found in the *Catechism of the Catholic Church* or other Church documents.[34]

4. The Connection Between Eucharist and Mission

Finally, the Emmaus story reminds us that the homily plays a key role in establishing the connection between the Eucharist and mission. Once they recognize the Risen Christ in "the breaking of the bread," the two disciples resolve to return to Jerusalem, despite the lateness of the hour, and rejoin the community they had left. In a word, they reverse direction and head back to where they should be going. There, along with the rest of the disciples, they encounter the Risen Christ anew and are given the mission of being his witnesses and preaching the Gospel of repentance and forgiveness to the world (Lk 24:36-49), a mission that would explode with power with the gift of the Spirit at Pentecost. This dimension of the Emmaus account corresponds to the "sending on mission" that concludes the Mass of the Roman Rite: "Go and announce the Gospel of the Lord."[35] Our encounter with Jesus inevitably leads to mission; our love for Jesus translates into our love for others. This is why the homily, which participates in the power of Christ's word, ought to inspire a sense of mission for those who hear it, making them doers and proclaimers of that same word in the world. A homily that does not lead to mission is, therefore, incomplete.

---

33   See CIC, c. 767 §1; CCEO, c. 614 §1.
34   See *Sacrosanctum Concilium*, no. 52; *Dei Verbum*, no. 24; CIC, c. 768; and CCEO, c. 616.
35   Excerpt from the English translation of *The Roman Missal* (International Committee on English in the Liturgy, Inc., 2010), 144.

II. THE MINISTRY OF LITURGICAL PREACHING

The Christological Foundation of the Homily

The Death and Resurrection of Jesus—the culmination and heart of Jesus' mission of revealing God's love for the world—is the central act of our salvation. And, as St. Paul writes citing a teaching that he himself had received and consequently counts as a foundational expression of tradition, "Christ died for our sins, according to the Scriptures," and "he rose again on the third day, according to the Scriptures" (1 Cor 15:3-4). The homilist, then, must again and again put into relief this "according to the Scriptures" of the Death and Resurrection of Jesus and its meaning for our lives. Every scriptural text on which he preaches leads to that center and sheds light on the mystery of that principal deed of God from different biblical perspectives—from some event in Israel's history (the first reading), from an apostle's theological reflection (the second reading), and from a particular Evangelist (the Gospel reading) who speaks of the life of Jesus in such a way as to show its climax in his Death and Resurrection.

As noted above, making this connection is what Jesus did for the two disciples on the road to Emmaus. The homilist should rely on the presence of the Risen Lord within him as he preaches, a presence guaranteed by the outpouring of the Spirit that he received in ordination. As the Risen Lord himself did, the homilist, "beginning with Moses and all the prophets," interprets for his congregation "what referred to him in all the Scriptures." And whatever is taught, the lesson is summarized in this way: "Was it not necessary that Christ should suffer these things and enter into his glory?" (Lk 24:26-27). Thus the person and mission of Jesus, culminating in his Death and Resurrection, is ultimately the central content of all the Scriptures.

The Essential Connection Between Scripture, the Homily, and the Eucharist

Looking at this fundamental pattern of preaching in the Emmaus narrative illustrates the essential connection between Scripture, the homily, and the Eucharist; for it was in the "breaking of the bread" that the disciples ultimately recognized their Risen Lord, and it was then they realized that their hearts were burning within them "while he spoke to us on the way and opened the Scriptures to us" (Lk 24:32). This is why virtually every homily preached during the liturgy should make some connection between the Scriptures just heard and the Eucharist about to be celebrated. Depending on what opportunities the texts in question provide, such a connection might be very brief or even only implicitly indicated, but at other times a firm connection should be established and drawn out. From the vantage point of Christian faith, the center of the Scriptures is the Death and Resurrection of Jesus, the ultimate sacrifice that brought redemption to the world. The sacrifice of the Eucharistic liturgy is the memorial of the Lord's Death, during the course of which we recognize that "the Lord has truly been raised" (Lk 24:34), is present to us and recognized by us in the breaking of the bread. When this connection is consistently made clear to the Christian people, they will understand the Scriptures and the mystery of the Eucharist ever more deeply. This is what the Council Fathers were speaking about when they said, "The Church has always venerated the divine Scriptures as she venerated the Body of the Lord, in so far as she never ceases, particularly in the sacred liturgy, to partake of the bread of life and to offer it to the faithful from the one table of the Word of God and the Body of Christ."[36]

Constructing homilies in such a way that this vision is actually achieved is, of course, a challenging project. But homilists should not be daunted by the task and should be encouraged by the grace of their ordination and by the great tradition of preaching that belongs to the whole Church. Their theological studies were geared toward helping them to move knowledgeably among the Scriptures[37] and to understand deeply the sacraments, which are

---

36 *Dei Verbum*, no. 21. See also *Presbyterorum Ordinis*, no. 18; *Sacrosanctum Concilium*, nos. 51, 56.
37 See *Sacrosanctum Concilium*, no. 24; CIC, c. 252 §2; CCEO, c. 350 §2.

so intimately joined to the Scriptures. There is no end to how much we can grow in the knowledge of these things.

The Sunday Homily, Doctrine, and the Church's Catechesis

The full scope of Jesus' preaching reminds us that when we have the privilege of preaching the homily to a congregation at the Sunday Eucharist, we also have an invaluable opportunity to advance the Church's catechetical ministry.[38] This intrinsic relationship between preaching, doctrine, and catechesis is also reflected in the ministry of Paul the Apostle. Paul describes himself as "compelled" to preach the Gospel: "For *everyone who calls on the name of the Lord will be saved*. But how can they call on him in whom they have not believed? And how can they believe in him of whom they have not heard? And how can they hear without someone to preach? And how can people preach unless they are sent? As it is written, *How beautiful are the feet of those who bring the good news!*" (Rom 10:13-16).

We do not have direct access to Paul's preaching, but interpreters of Paul have noted the liturgical context of his letters. Paul's letters were most likely read in the liturgical assemblies of the early Christian communities. While his letters are not Sunday homilies as such, they are, in a sense, an "extended homily," with the bearer of the letter communicating Paul's teaching contained therein to his communities and perhaps amplifying Paul's message in doing so. Paul's letters show evidence of this liturgical setting, typically opening with greetings and prayers of thanksgiving and praise (e.g., Rom 1:8-10; 1 Cor 1:4-9) and concluding with words of blessing (e.g., Rom 16:25-27; 2 Cor 13:13). Parts of early Christian hymns are also found in his letters (e.g., Phil 2:6-11).

For Paul, the heart of his apostolic preaching is the mystery of Christ, especially the central mystery of the Death and Resurrection of Christ. Paul's proclamation focuses on the initial gift of salvation in Christ freely given to us through faith in Christ: "But God proves his love for us in that while we were still sinners Christ died for us" (Rom 5:8). Paul's purpose is to draw his hearers into full awareness of the depth of that mystery in which they

---

38   See CCC, no.1074: "[The liturgy] is therefore the privileged place for catechizing the People of God."

have already been plunged through Baptism. Paul's words of thanksgiving for Christians remind them of their own call to new life in Christ: "I give thanks to my God always on your account for the grace of God bestowed on you in Christ Jesus, that in him you were enriched in every way, with all discourse and all knowledge, as the testimony to Christ was confirmed among you, so that you are not lacking in any spiritual gift as you wait for the revelation of our Lord Jesus Christ" (1 Cor 1:4-7).

But Paul also spends considerable time in his letters illustrating how faith in Christ and participation in the life of the Church have an impact on the totality of Christian life, offering, as it were, an extended catechetical presentation for his communities. Indeed, in two separate places Paul's letters identify the express purpose of his ministry of the word: to "present everyone perfect in Christ" (Col 1:28) and "so that one who belongs to God may be competent, equipped for every good work" (2 Tm 3:17). He more than once contrasts a life lived according to the "flesh" with that lived according to the "Spirit" (e.g., Rom 8:1-13). In his Letter to the Philippians, Paul argues against divisions and factions in the community by appealing to the profound humility of Jesus himself, who did not cling to his divine status but became flesh for us, even to dying on the Cross (see Phil 2:1-5). In his first Letter to the Corinthians, Paul responds to a number of practical questions and problems presented by Christians (factions, marital problems, immorality in the community, how to respond to the issue of eating meat offered to idols, and so on) by spelling out what kind of behavior life in Christ demands.

Paul also deals extensively with what we could call doctrinal issues, as for example, in responding to the Christians' questions about life beyond death (1 Thes 4:13-18; 2 Cor 5:1-10; and 1 Cor 15) or the nature of the Eucharist (1 Cor 11:17-34). In the latter two instances, Paul cites the early Church's creedal tradition about Jesus' Death and Resurrection that he himself had received and now passes on to his community (1 Cor 11:23-26; 15:3-5). Paul also urges his fellow Christians to immerse themselves in the life of the Spirit, to pray always (1 Thes 5:17), and to sing spiritual hymns and prayers of praise to God (Col 3:16). He also exhorts the Christians to encourage one another, to be bound together in affirming and respectful speech, to use their diverse gifts in harmony, to love one another and thus build up the Church as the Body of Christ (see especially 1 Cor 12-14).

This same pattern in Paul's proclamation of the Christian message— announcing the mysteries of redemption and then drawing out the meaning of these mysteries for Christian life—is vividly illustrated in the Letter to the Ephesians, a text that may have been intended as a later summation of the Apostle's teaching. The epistle begins with an acclamation of praise that God has chosen to reveal to the followers of Jesus the mystery of his will, the mystery of God's redemptive love revealed in the Death and Resurrection of Jesus, and the forgiveness and reconciliation that flows from that divine source (Eph 1:3-10). From that foundation, Ephesians goes on to consider the reconciling work of Christ, who through his Death on the Cross makes peace, bringing together both Gentile and Jew into one new person by breaking down the wall of enmity between them. And further still, from that cosmic vision of God's redemptive and reconciling love, the epistle derives the necessity of unity within the Church herself as the Body of Christ and sets forth her mission of proclaiming God's reconciling love to the world. Thus Paul believed that the initial grace of faith in Christ was meant to transform the entirety of one's existence, and therefore in his preaching he reflected at some length on what Christian life should mean for those to whom he preached the Gospel.

Certainly, doctrine is not meant to be propounded in a homily in the way that it might unfold in a theology classroom or a lecture for an academic audience or even a catechism lesson. The homily is integral to the liturgical act of the Eucharist, and the language and spirit of the homily should fit that context. Yet catechesis in its broadest sense involves the effective communication of the full scope of the Church's teaching and formation, from initiation into the Sacrament of Baptism through the moral requirements of a faithful Christian life. As the Catechism of the Catholic Church notes, "Catechesis is an education in the faith of children, young people, and adults which includes especially the teaching of Christian doctrine imparted, generally speaking, in an organic and systematic way, with a view to initiating the hearers into the fullness of Christian life."[39] The Catechism itself is organized into four "pillars" of Christian life, reflecting on the Creed, the celebration of the Christian mystery in our liturgical and sacramental life, the moral responsibilities of life in Christ, and finally, the meaning of Christian prayer.

Over time the homilist, while respecting the unique form and spirit of the Sunday homily, should communicate the full scope of this rich catechetical teaching to his congregation. During the course of the liturgical year it

---

39   CCC, no. 5.

is appropriate to offer the faithful, prudently and on the basis of the three-year Lectionary, "'thematic' homilies treating the great themes of the Christian faith."[40] Consequently, diocesan bishops may offer occasional suggested themes for Sunday homilies in their own dioceses in order to guide the teaching of the faithful by the clergy and to ensure effective and timely catechetical preaching on significant pastoral concerns, while at the same time preserving the importance of preaching on liturgical seasons and the texts of the *Lectionary for Mass*. It would also be helpful for experts and publishers to prepare pastoral aids for the clergy to help connect the proclamation of the readings with the doctrines of the Church. The beautiful words of Ephesians express this apostolic longing to communicate the full sense of the Christian mystery: " . . . that Christ may dwell in your hearts through faith; that you, rooted and grounded in love, may have strength to comprehend with all the holy ones what is the breadth and length and height and depth, and to know the love of Christ that surpasses knowledge, so that you may be filled with all the fullness of God" (Eph 3:17-19).

Therefore a wedge should not be driven between the proper content and style of the Sunday homily and the teaching of the Church's doctrine. To encounter the living presence of the Risen Christ in the word of the Scriptures and in the Sacrament of his Body and Blood is not incompatible with effective communication of what faith in Christ means for our lives. Without being pedantic, overly abstract, or theoretical, the homilist can effectively spell out, for example, the connection between Jesus' care for the poor and the Church's social teaching and concern for the common good; or Jesus' pronouncements on the prohibition of divorce and the Church's teaching on the sacredness of the marriage bond; or Jesus' confrontations with his opponents and the Church's obligation to challenge contemporary culture about the values that should define our public life.

Making a thoughtful and integral connection between the Scripture passages proclaimed in the Eucharist and the requirements of Christian belief and life should also be keyed to the seasons of the liturgical year: reflection on the ultimate purpose and direction of our lives in the Advent season; the gift of life and the joy of the Incarnation at the Christmas season; the need for repentance and renewal during Lent; the dynamic gift of the Spirit in our lives at Pentecost. We know, too, that at certain moments in the liturgical

---

40   *Sacramentum Caritatis*, no. 46.

year, such as Christmas or Easter, the assembly will likely include many Catholics who participate only occasionally in the Church's liturgy. Although not in the context of Sunday worship, similar pastoral opportunities are present at weddings or funerals, when family members who may have strayed from the practice of their faith are present at these moments of family joy and sorrow. This is obviously not the time to chide such Catholics for their absence. Rather, the homilist should use the beauty of the liturgy and the contents of the homily to open the Scriptures, to make a gracious and thoughtful connection to the meaning of Christian faith in the world today, and to invite back those who have lost contact with the Church. This is precisely the rationale of the call for a New Evangelization of those Catholics who, for whatever reason, have drifted away from their spiritual home. Through the prayerful celebration of the Eucharistic ritual and through the graceful and respectful proclamation of the word, all are invited to be aware of their deepest spiritual and human longings and to immerse themselves again in the mystery of Christ present in the Eucharist, who alone is able to quench their deepest spiritual thirst.

The doctrines of the Church should direct the homilist and ensure that he arrives at and preaches about what is in fact the deepest meaning of Scripture and sacrament for Christian life. For doctrines simply formulate with accuracy what the Church, prompted by the gift of the Spirit, has come to know through the Scriptures proclaimed in the believing assembly and through the sacraments that are celebrated on the foundation of these Scriptures.

The most central mysteries of our faith—the Trinity, the Incarnation, and the redemption that Christ reveals in his Paschal Sacrifice—were attested in the Scriptures and are proclaimed and celebrated in the Eucharist. They were formulated with precision over time by the Church's Magisterium to keep the communities that read the Scriptures and celebrated the Eucharist in the same communion of right understanding and right worship (*orthodoxy*) about these things, a communion that was to hold across the whole world and through the centuries. For that same reason these doctrines ought to be seamlessly introduced and articulated still today in the course of our liturgical celebrations in order to ensure that by reading the Scriptures and celebrating the Eucharist we understand ever more deeply the essential beliefs of the Church.[41]

One effective way to do this might be to connect some point of the homily to a phrase or key idea of the Creed that will be immediately recited by the assembly when the homily is finished. The Creed has the same center that the Scriptures and the Eucharist have. It is that the "one Lord Jesus Christ . . . suffered death and was buried, and rose again on the third day in accordance with the Scriptures." But this Jesus is "true God from true God, begotten, not made, consubstantial with the Father." The homilist proclaims and teaches that this is the one "who came down from heaven, and by the Holy Spirit was incarnate of the Virgin Mary, and became man." This is the one whom we see moving about, speaking and acting in the Gospels. This is the one who "suffered death and was buried and rose again." We see here what St. Cyril of Jerusalem meant when, in handing over the Creed to those who would soon be baptized, he explained, "The most important doctrines were collected from the whole of Scripture to make a single exposition of the faith."[42]

So, when all is said and done, why should the homilist preach doctrinally and catechetically? Because, as Paul and the Evangelists knew, the people are drawn to Jesus and his Gospel by the beauty and truth of the mysteries of our faith. The ultimate goal of proclaiming the Gospel is to lead people into a loving and intimate relationship with the Lord, a relationship that forms the character of their persons and guides them in living out their faith. A good homilist, for example, is able to articulate the mystery of the Incarnation—that the eternal Son of God came to dwell among us as man—in such a manner that his listeners are able to understand more deeply the beauty and truth of this mystery and to see its connections with daily life. By highlighting his humanity, his poverty, his compassion, his forthrightness, and his suffering and Death, an effective homily would show the faithful just how much the Son of God loved them in taking our flesh upon himself. And by expanding the congregation's love for the humanity of Jesus, the homilist could also move his fellow Christians to a deeper sense of justice, with a sense of compassion for the most vulnerable and the poor and of the broken humanity of

---

41 The CCC expresses this well (no. 170): "We do not believe in formulas, but in those realities they express, which faith allows us to touch . . . All the same, we do approach these realities with the help of formulations of the faith which permit us to express the faith and to hand it on, to celebrate it in community, to assimilate and live on it more and more." See also CIC, cc. 760, 767 §1, 768, 769; and CCEO, cc. 614 §1, 616.
42 Cyril of Jerusalem, *Catechesis* 5:12, 1.

their neighbors. Likewise, a homilist could speak about Christ's Real Presence in the Eucharist in a way that draws upon the Catholic doctrinal tradition of transubstantiation, underlining the significance of this awe-inspiring presence of the Risen Christ in our midst. Our Catholic piety and reverence in the liturgy could be explained by our dramatic belief in God's fulfillment of his promise to be one with us. As the homilist points to the experience of our communion with God, he could draw attention to our bond of communion with each other.

Of course, what is essential for speaking about the mysteries of our faith with passion and conviction is that the preacher himself grasps the doctrinal significance of their truth and so loves these mysteries himself that he can communicate that love and truth to his listeners.

The Role of Scripture in the Homily

An effective homily takes its cue from the very nature of the Scriptures themselves, which use a rich variety of literary forms to communicate their message: narratives, metaphors, hymns, prayers, proverbial sayings, and poetry all have their place within the pages of the Bible. These stories and sayings of the Bible have had a profound influence over time on the Christian imagination, and indeed still have an impact on popular culture itself. Like good poetry, the Scriptures give us the language to express our deepest hopes and longings, to find the right words for our grief and loss, our moments of joy and peace, our attempts to thank and praise God.

A prime example is, in fact, Jesus' own preaching. Matthew's Gospel, for instance, portrays Jesus on a boat near the shore, teaching the vast crowds that follow him in parables, those pointed stories that were characteristic of Jesus' preaching ministry (see Mt 13:1-53). The discourse begins with the parable of the sower (13:1-9), which Jesus would later explain to his disciples (13:18-23). The seeds fall on various types of soil, determining the outcome of the harvest; Jesus will use the sower parable to identify the kinds of conditions and responses necessary for the "word of the kingdom" to thrive. Jesus goes on to use a profusion of other images and brief stories to illustrate aspects of the Kingdom of Heaven: a field in which an enemy sows weeds among the wheat and the lesson that the two should remain together in our complex world until the harvest; a tiny mustard seed that grows into a large bush where the birds of the sky come and dwell in its branches; the yeast that a woman mixes with three measures of wheat flour and that manages to leaven all of it; a man finding a treasure in a field and selling everything he has to purchase the field (and its treasure); a merchant who finds a "pearl of great price" and sells all that he has to purchase it; and, finally, the story of the dragnet that, when thrown into the sea, collects "fish of every kind": when it is hauled to shore, the fish have to be sorted and the good fish put into buckets.

This remarkable abundance of images and stories, all found in only one chapter of Matthew's Gospel, tells us that Jesus was not an abstract preacher but laced his preaching with rich images and provocative stories. The images and examples are drawn from the agrarian context in which his audiences in first-century Galilee lived and from the fishing industry that thrived around the Sea of Galilee, where most of Jesus' ministry took place. As natural storytellers usually are, Jesus was a keen observer of human life, with all of its beauty and complexity. His metaphors and stories have a poetic and unforgettable spirit and have worked their way into the literature of every human generation since.

But Jesus was not content simply to cite ordinary examples; there is in Jesus' parables a quality of strangeness, something out of the ordinary, that grips the imagination and triggers wonderment on the part of the hearer: the incredible bounty of the harvest ("hundred or sixty or thirtyfold"), the amazing size of the bush that blossoms from a tiny mustard seed, the huge amount of flour that is leavened ("three measures," estimated at sixty pounds—enough bread to feed a village!), the radical act of selling everything one has to buy the treasure in the field or the pearl of great price.

The special power of the parable is to engage the listener about its meaning. Artful human speech, especially in stories, can appear to veil truth for those who do not engage it and yet can reveal truth for those willing to listen and ponder its meaning. Some cultures in particular relish stories that bring home to them the practical wisdom of the Gospel. Jesus did not simply lecture his audiences but enticed them by evoking experiences they were invited to think about and try to understand. Being an effective storyteller may not be a gift that comes easily to everyone who must preach, but the lesson here is that the homilist must have empathy for human experience, observe it closely and sympathetically, and incorporate it into his preaching.[43]

The goal of the homily is to lead the hearer to the deep inner connection between God's word and the actual circumstances of one's everyday life. In some instances one's own experience—told in an appropriate way without drawing too much attention to oneself—can also be effective, especially when this experience is one that resonates with similar experiences of those with whom it is shared. Pope Benedict XVI makes this very point: "The homily is a means of bringing the scriptural message to life in a way that helps the faithful to realize that God's word is present and at work in their everyday lives. . . . Consequently, those who have been charged with preaching by virtue of a specific ministry ought to take this task to heart. Generic and abstract homilies which obscure the directness of God's word should be avoided, as well as useless digressions which risk drawing greater attention to the preacher than to the heart of the Gospel message."[44]

However, the homilist cannot be content simply to repeat the biblical language found in the readings but must open its meaning and help illumine the experience of those who hear the biblical word. The homily is intended to establish a "dialogue" between the sacred biblical text and the Christian life of the hearer. The homily in its most effective form enables the hearer to understand the meaning of the Scriptures in a new way and, in turn, helps the message of the Scriptures, proclaimed in the context of the liturgy, to illumine the experience of the hearer. Thus the homily brings together both the biblical message and the contemporary experience of those to whom the homily is offered. Apt stories that illustrate human experience or the realities of contemporary culture help enliven the homily and open avenues for understanding the meaning of the biblical text, which comes from an ancient

---

43 The role of reflection on experience was a particular emphasis of *Fulfilled in Your Hearing*: "In order to make such connections between the lives of the people and the Gospel, the preacher will have to be a listener before he is a speaker. Listening is not an isolated moment. It is a way of life. It means openness to the Lord's voice not only in the Scriptures but in the events of our daily lives and in the experience of our brothers and sisters" (10).

44 *Verbum Domini*, no. 59.

time and culture but still has the capacity to transcend the chasm of time and to touch, inspire, and challenge the contemporary Christian.

The Homily as an Ecclesial Act

We should also note that the preaching of a homily, since it occurs in the context of the Church's liturgy, is by definition a profound ecclesial act, one that should be in evident communion with the Church's Magisterium and with the consciousness that one stands in the midst of a community of faith. The homily is not an isolated example of biblical interpretation or a purely academic exercise. It is directed *from* faith, that of the Church and of the ordained minister who preaches in the name of Christ and his Church, *to* faith—that is, the faith of the Christian community gathered in a spirit of prayer and praise in the presence of the Risen Christ. Thus the words of the homilist should be in harmony with the spirit and teaching of the Church. While the homily should be respectful of those who hear it and therefore be thoughtful, well-prepared, and coherent, the Sunday homily is not a time for theological speculation. It is a sacred ecclesial act meant to lead from the biblical word to the Eucharistic action and thereby to nourish faith and build up the Body of Christ gathered in prayer. This ecclesial sensitivity in liturgical preaching was a hallmark of the Church Fathers, many of whose extant writings are in fact the record of their preaching.

Fidelity to the Church's Magisterium does not mean, however, that the homily should be an abstract affirmation of doctrine. The purpose and spirit of the homily is to inspire and move those who hear it, to enable them to understand in heart and mind what the mysteries of our redemption mean for our lives and how they might call us to repentance and change. Here again we can find wisdom in Jesus' own example. One of the most enticing scenes in the Gospels is Jesus' encounter with the Samaritan woman in John's Gospel (Jn 4:4-42), a passage provided in the Lectionary as appropriate for the rite of preparation of adult candidates for Baptism.

John tells us that Jesus, making his way from Jerusalem to Galilee, passed through the region of Samaria. Tired from his journey, he sat down by a well associated with the Patriarch Jacob. Samaria was a place that Jews typically avoided, yet John presents Jesus, the Good Shepherd (Jn 10:11), as not hesitating to extend his mission to this region. To the well, at the hottest time of the day, comes a Samaritan woman. John relates how the ensuing dialogue of

Jesus with the Samaritan woman is both challenging and respectful, probing yet tender and filled with understanding, as the Master offers this woman the gift of divine life, living water that will forever slake her thirst.

There are dimensions of Jesus' encounter with the Samaritan woman that are important for effective homiletic preaching, especially its catechetical dimension. In the course of their conversation, Jesus makes a blunt demand: "Go call your husband and come back" (Jn 4:16). The woman responds without hesitation that she has no husband, and Jesus, in an artful, almost playful way, concurs: "You are right in saying, 'I have no husband.' For you have had five husbands, and the one you have now is not your husband" (Jn 4:18). His moral judgment could not be clearer and more direct, but the woman is able to hear it receptively precisely because of the sensitivity and respect Jesus shows her, reflective of Jesus' respect for women illustrated throughout the Gospels.

Jesus' conversation with the Samaritan woman shows us that moral challenges presented by the Church's teaching—such as those in this Gospel story dealing with the delicate issues of sexuality, marriage, and relationships—can be offered and can be heard, provided that they are made in the context of the promise of grace. Some ethnic groups, for example, are reluctant to speak openly with each other about sexual matters, yet there is a need to do so in a reverent and thoughtful manner. The homilist can artfully inspire this by recalling the beauty and dignity of human sexuality, by recalling the respect owed one's spouse, by challenging the often crude and exploitative discourse about sexuality that pervades our contemporary world, and by recalling the teaching of the Church on the sacredness of the body and the meaning of marriage.

The woman at the well was not put off by Jesus' willingness to confront her situation; indeed, it drew from her a word of praise: "Sir, I can see that you are a prophet" (Jn 4:19). It was Jesus' manner, his willingness to communicate with the woman and listen to her with respect, that enabled him to speak with her about the difficulties of her life.

This example from John's Gospel demonstrates that preaching the word of God should reveal God's enlivening and forgiving grace, engage human experience with respect and care, and address in a truthful and proper way the realities of sin and human frailty. Jesus' conversation with the woman at the well led her to a renewed life and a sense of joy and purpose. So the Sunday homily—involving inspiration, information, and moral instruction—is meant to lead finally to the right praise of God, to true "thanksgiving," which is at the heart of the Liturgy of the Eucharist.

Nearly all parish communities include women and men who have been harmed emotionally and spiritually by an abortion experience. While reminding the community of the beauty and sacredness of human life, the homilist should always emphasize God's infinite mercy for all sinners, including those suffering after an abortion. Like the woman at the well, such individuals need to be invited to approach the Church without fear, in order to receive God's forgiveness and healing grace.

III. THE ONE ORDAINED TO PREACH

The Preacher as a Man of Holiness

To preach the Gospel authentically to the Christian community, the homilist should strive to live a life of holiness. In the Gospel according to Matthew, Jesus strongly challenges those religious leaders who "preach but . . . do not practice," those who "tie up heavy burdens hard to carry and lay them on people's shoulders, but . . . will not lift a finger to move them" (Mt 23:3-4). To attempt to evangelize through words and example those who need to revitalize their faith, without awareness of one's own need for ongoing spiritual renewal, would be in vain. The homilist who humbly and confidently seeks the light and inspiration of the Holy Spirit in the preparation of the homily proclaims God's word with greater clarity, integrity, and effectiveness. This in turn enables him and the hearers to participate more fully and actively, with more understanding and authentic faith, in the Eucharist.

Indeed the time given to preparing the homily must begin with a fruitful time of reflection and prayer. Just as the celebration of the Eucharistic liturgy itself is not a theatrical performance or simply a matter of the rituals being correctly carried out, neither is the homily simply an exercise in good public speaking. Along with the study and care given to the content of the homily and the manner of its presentation, there should also be time for personal reflection on the meaning of the Scriptures and scrutiny of one's own spiritual life in prayerful silence. As Pope Benedict XVI notes in *Verbum Domini*, "Preachers need to be in close and constant contact with the sacred text; they should prepare for the homily by meditation and prayer, so as to preach with conviction and passion."[45] In this sense, the evangelizer must also first make sure that his own life has engaged the power of the Gospel of Jesus Christ.

---

45   *Verbum Domini*, no. 59.

Quoting St. Augustine, the pope observes, "He is undoubtedly barren who preaches outwardly the word of God without hearing it inwardly."[46]

Especially for the preacher, the commitment to prayer also entails praying with and on behalf of the people to whom he preaches. The true pastor and good shepherd knows his people's sorrows, their anxieties, their weaknesses, their capacity for love, their abiding joys, and their deepest longings.[47] Only when the homilist, in a spirit of faith and love, is conscious of his own deepest experience and those of his people can he preach persuasively to them.

The Preacher as a Man of Scripture

As one whose duty is to proclaim the word of God, the homilist must necessarily be a person with a deep love of the Scriptures and one whose spirituality is profoundly shaped by God's word.[48] This entails being someone who habitually immerses himself in the language, stories, rhythms, speech patterns, and ethos of the Scriptures. The words of the Bible should be readily at hand and often on his lips; he should commit important passages of Scripture to memory and have a sure grasp of the narrative thrust of the entire Bible. His Bible should be near at hand, carrying it with him when he travels or perhaps staying linked to it by computer or other mobile technology. He may bring it with him when he prays before the Blessed Sacrament. Moreover, every preacher should regularly consult good scriptural commentaries, both of the technical and "spiritual" type. Also to be recommended are the homilies and biblical commentaries of the Church Fathers, especially those of Origen, St. Augustine, St. Ephrem, St. John Chrysostom, and St. Jerome.

As noted above, a particularly effective means of immersing oneself prayerfully in the biblical texts is the ancient practice of *lectio divina*, a discipline that includes attentive and prayerful reading of the Scriptures and contemplation about their meaning for one's life—an approach warmly recommended by Pope Benedict XVI in *Verbum Domini*.[49]

The whole point of these methods and practices is that the preacher learns to see the world through biblical eyes. He should become adept at noticing the analogies between the Bible and ordinary experience so that he

---

46 *Verbum Domini*, no. 59.
47 See CIC, c. 529 §1.
48 See *Presbyterorum Ordinis*, no. 4.
49 See *Verbum Domini*, nos. 86-87.

can illumine the latter through recourse to the former. The birth of a child today is an echo of the Birth of Christ; a time of suffering in the hospital right now is in some way connected to the suffering of Jesus on the Cross; a summons to a vocation heard by a young woman in a parish is not unlike the call heard by Mary of Nazareth from the angel Gabriel; a failure of integrity by a business executive is reminiscent of the Israelites' failure in the desert; a struggle for justice in our society is supported by Amos's cry of protest on behalf of the poor, and so on. Thereby the Scriptures give voice to our deepest longings and aspirations.

The Preacher as a Man of Tradition

Along with a profound love of the Scriptures the homilist should also have knowledge of and religious adherence to the Church's Sacred Tradition and its essential link to Scripture. From the perspective of Catholic faith, the one word of God is expressed both in Scripture and in the Church's Tradition.[50] Blessed John Henry Newman said that the teaching of the Bible is like a seed, which has gradually unfolded across space and through time.[51] Theology, spirituality, the liturgy, the lives of the saints, the formal teaching of the Church, great Catholic art, architecture, and poetry—all of these constitute the unfolding of the word of God within our Catholic heritage. Tradition along with Scripture, therefore, is an important source from which preachers can draw inspiration.[52] Preachers should have the *habitus* of theology: the steady practice of reading the theological masters (both ancient and modern) and meditating on the great questions that they entertain. They should cultivate a real love for the writings of the doctors of the Church and study with eagerness the manner in which the Church's life and teaching have developed.

The Preacher as a Man of Communion

Effective preaching also entails a thoughtful and informed understanding of contemporary culture. The Fathers of the Second Vatican Council made this

50   See *Dei Verbum*, nos. 9-10.
51   Blessed John Henry Newman, *An Essay of the Development of Christian Doctrine* (New York: Christian Classics Inc., 1968), 80.
52   CIC, c. 760.

point when they insisted that leaders within the Catholic Church must be deeply attuned, not only to Scripture and Tradition, but also to the "signs of the times," signals coming from today's world. As noted in the preface to *Gaudium et Spes*, "The joy and hope, the grief and anguish of the men of our time, especially of those who are poor or afflicted in any way, are the joy and hope, the grief and anguish of the followers of Christ as well. Nothing that is genuinely human fails to find an echo in their hearts."[53] This is the spirit of "communion" that Pope John Paul II noted belongs to the exercise of priesthood: "Within the Church's life the priest is a man of communion, in his relations with all people he must be a man of mission and dialogue. Deeply rooted in the truth and charity of Christ, and impelled by the desire and imperative to proclaim Christ's salvation to all, the priest is called to witness in all his relationships to fraternity, service and a common quest for the truth, as well as a concern for the promotion of justice and peace."[54]

It would be inappropriate for the homilist to impose on the congregation his own partisan views about current issues. Yet for preaching to be so abstract that it reveals no awareness of or concern for the great economic and social issues that are affecting people's lives in a serious way would give the impression that the words of Scripture and the action of the Eucharist are without relevance for our everyday experience and our human hopes and dreams.[55] Preachers should be aware, in an appropriate way, of what their people are watching on television, what kind of music they are listening to, which websites they find appealing, and which films they find compelling. References to these more popular cultural expressions—which at times can be surprisingly replete with religious motifs—can be an effective way to engage the interest of those on the edge of faith.

The population of the United States is marked by extraordinary diversity. Even within the Catholic Church the liturgical, theological, and spiritual traditions of the various Eastern Catholic Churches are different from those of the Latin Church. Yet all these traditions of the East and the West are of equal dignity and are essential components of the one Catholic Church. The Eastern Churches that are in full communion are often characterized as "ancient" and "venerable," because they draw in a special way on the teaching

---

53 *Gaudium et Spes* (*Pastoral Constitution on the Church in the Modern World*), no. 1.
54 Blessed John Paul II, *Pastores Dabo Vobis* (*I Will Give You Shepherds*), no. 18.
55 The Church's social doctrine is an indispensable aid in helping the preacher apply the Scriptures and clarify the moral and ethical implications of the social and political order (see *Compendium of the Social Doctrine of the Church*).

and spirit of the early Church Fathers. The Patristic writings are a primary resource for proclamation in the Eastern Churches; each of them has a treasury of outstanding preachers who share in the common mission to proclaim the word of God within the celebration of the divine liturgy.

In the last fifty years, our country has received substantial numbers of immigrants from Mexico, the Caribbean, Central America, South America, the Middle East, Eastern Europe, Vietnam, the Philippines, India, China, Nigeria, Uganda, Tanzania, and many other places. This influx of peoples has made the United States one of the most culturally diverse countries on the planet, and a very significant number of these new immigrants are Catholics. The Church in the United States has benefited greatly from the cultural wealth and diversity of experience that these new immigrants have brought to our shores. In many cases, the presence of Asian, Latin American, Eastern European, and African Catholics has meant new life for parishes that had been fragile. So much diversity is both an opportunity and a challenge for any preacher.

Particular cultures often have their own preferences for which style of preaching they find most compelling. Take, for example, the tradition of preaching in African American communities.[56] The fruit of a rich and fertile past, this tradition has matured into an actual style and art of delivering a homily. In the African American experience of preaching, the style of the homily often becomes more interactive between the homilist and the assembly, with the assembly often making a response from their hearts: "Amen!"; "Yes, Lord!"; "Thank you, Jesus!" As *In Spirit and in Truth* reminds us, "Traditionally, good 'Black preaching' is rich in content and expression, relies heavily on the biblical text, and draws generously from story, song, poetry, humor, anecdote, and descriptive language. . . . The homily must enable the community to worship God with praise and thanksgiving."[57]

Once he has come to know the customs, mores, practices, history, and religiosity of a people, a homilist can draw on that richness in order to make his presentation of the faith fresh and enlivening. Moreover, by examining a culture or Catholic ritual tradition other than his own, he can learn different expressions of the one Catholic faith, and this can only enhance his own appropriation of the faith and his presentation of it to others. Learning a new

---

56   See *Plenty Good Room: The Spirit and Truth of African American Worship* (Washington, DC: USCCB, 1990).
57   *In Spirit and in Truth: Black Catholic Reflections on the Order of the Mass* (USCCB, 2005), no. 35.

language can give an entirely new texture to his words and ideas, enabling him to express the mystery of the Gospel in a compelling manner.

At the same time, cultural complexity poses a sharp challenge to the preacher in the effort to communicate the faith to people, because he may not share their education, background, and assumptions. Pastoral ministry, and especially the ministry of preaching, challenges the ordained minister to have a deep respect for other cultures and, to the extent possible, to enter into another culture with humility, attention, and deep love. He should strive, above all, to learn the language of the people he serves and, as best he can, to appreciate their manner of thinking, feeling, and acting. Only then can he preach heart to heart. Also, he ought never to forget that, despite enormous differences among us at the level of language, practice, history, lifestyle, and social class, we remain, in spiritual essentials, one. Everyone wants joy in life, but at times sadness strikes; everyone is finite and yet has expansive hopes and longings; everyone seeks friendship but also experiences times of loneliness and isolation; everyone sins; everyone is a subject worthy of respect; and everyone is called by God. The liturgical assembly is challenged also. It must make the extra effort to listen attentively to homilists for whom English is not their first language. Listeners of the homily ought to welcome the wisdom offered by these preachers. The homilist speaking to a culture not his own can find encouragement in the Christian communion in which he and his people share, a unity meant to be celebrated in the Eucharist itself.

Although the Catholic population in the United States is blessed with many different cultures, the Hispanic/Latino segment of the Catholic community is growing at a particularly rapid rate and poses substantial opportunities and challenges for effective preaching in this context.[58] Many Hispanic Catholics are especially attuned to the symbolic and sacramental world of Catholicism. Successful preachers who may come from a different cultural context would do well to immerse themselves in Hispanic popular piety, a world in which Mary and the saints are venerated with intense fervor and affection and in which there is profound devotion to the Virgin Mary and the suffering Christ. Popular religiosity should not be looked down upon,

---

58   See *Encuentro and Mission: A Renewed Pastoral Framework for Hispanic Ministry* (USCCB, 2002) concerning the particular urgency needed for the Church in the United States to respond properly to the growing Hispanic/Latino Catholic population.

and the homilist should learn from it and relate to it with respect and sensitivity.[59] This requires exposure to the people's neighborhoods or *barrios*, their homes and associations, and even their countries of origin, if at all possible. As with any cultural group, people appreciate pastors and preachers who cultivate personal relationships with them and demonstrate a willingness to move beyond their comfort zones and enter the world of the "other." In this regard Spanish-language ability is an urgent need. Opportunities for pastoral immersion experiences in Latin America can also have an important formative impact. Seminaries and permanent diaconate formation programs are urged to include Spanish-language preparation and proper exposure to Hispanic cultures into their programs of priestly formation.[60]

Of particular relevance for preachers who wish to connect with these congregations are the serious social, economic, and political struggles of the Hispanic/Latino poor. The Church in the United States, like U.S. society as a whole, is characterized by a growing gap between those who are well off and can live comfortably, and a significant working class—many of them Hispanic/Latino—who increasingly find it difficult to make ends meet. Hispanics face daunting issues such as a lack of access to education and medical care, crime, poor housing, youth at risk, and immigration concerns. The effective preacher will be aware of and acknowledge people's struggle for a better life in the United States and in their countries of origin.

At the same time, however, the homily should not replicate civic or political discourse. Especially in the context of the Eucharist, people want to hear God's word robustly and reverently proclaimed. The preacher is successful if he plumbs the depths of the Scripture and, when appropriate, recalls stories about Mary and the saints. The people want the preacher to witness to

---

59 See *Sacrosanctum Concilium*, no. 13; *Lumen Gentium* (*Dogmatic Constitution on the Church*), no. 67; *Marialis Cultus* (*www.vatican.va/holy_father/paul_vi/apost_exhortations/documents/ hf_p-vi_exh_19740202_marialis-cultus_en.html*), nos. 30-31; and the Congregation for Divine Worship and the Discipline of the Sacraments, *Directory on Popular Piety and the Liturgy: Principles and Guidelines* (*www.vatican.va/roman_curia/congregations/ccdds/documents/ rc_con_ccdds_doc_20020513_vers-direttorio_en.html*).

60 "Seminarians must learn Spanish and become familiar with Hispanic culture. Also, provide clergy and religious with opportunities to learn Spanish and to gain an understanding of the customs, cultures, and histories of Latin America. This is no longer an option—it is a need" (*Encuentro and Mission*, no. 55, 2c); PPF, 5th edition, nos. 172, 182, 189, and 228.

God's presence and power as displayed in miracles and other manifestations of divine transcendence.

For immigrant groups—most notably Hispanic/Latino—an important issue is the heightened tension between parents and children around issues of assimilation. Preachers need to be sensitive to the process by which parents convey the faith to new generations, who often know little Spanish (or other particular language of origin). Good preaching honors the experience of immigrant families and sympathizes with the challenges of adapting to life in the United States. In this regard preaching must reflect insight into the Church's evangelizing mission, which requires cultural discernment based on gospel values that go beyond those of any particular culture. Preaching in Hispanic/Latino contexts requires familiarity with the policy of ecclesial integration as distinct from assimilation, which has been specified in USCCB documents.[61] In the context of adjustment to a new culture and way of life, preaching among Hispanic/Latino and other non-European communities correlates with the Church's overarching goal of communion in diversity. In certain pastoral circumstances, bilingual or multilingual preaching may be a good option to ensure that all in the congregation understand the homily.

The increasing presence of international priests in the pastoral life of the United States is a great blessing but also requires sustained efforts at cultural and linguistic adaptation, particularly in relationship to effective preaching. Dioceses and religious communities need to offer these brother priests opportunities for intense language preparation and help in understanding the varied social and pastoral contexts of Catholics in this country.

Speaking with Respect and Reverence for Others

The unique opportunity to address an entire congregation with the innate authority of the preacher in the Sunday homily also requires sensitivity and respect when speaking of other Christians or other religious traditions. A spirit of respect based on a sound knowledge of their traditions should characterize observations in homilies about Orthodox or Protestant Christians, with whom we enjoy a real, if imperfect, communion. After all, Orthodox

---

61   See *Encuentro and Mission*, no. 38.

Christians are linked with us in the "closest intimacy"[62] by the same sacraments, including the Eucharist and Holy Orders. Protestant Christians, too, are our brothers and sisters in Christ, based on a common Baptism and a reverence for the Scriptures, and have a preaching tradition from which we have much to learn. This common Christian identity must always provide the context when speaking of other Christians in homilies, especially when commenting on specific differences.

The diversity of the American population and the tensions within contemporary society should also alert the preacher to the need for respect and a thoughtful use of language when speaking of other faith communities in the Sunday homily. A succession of statements by modern popes and U.S. bishops, for example, has emphasized the need to avoid any prejudice or anti-Jewish or anti-Semitic views in Catholic preaching. Proclamation of the Scriptures should be, if anything, an occasion for promoting respect for Judaism and the Jewish tradition, the spiritual ancestry from which Jesus and the Gospels emerged.[63]

The political turbulence and violence in the Middle East sometimes contributes to local prejudice against Muslims in our country. It is important to remind the faithful that, as stated clearly in *Nostra Aetate*,[64] recent papal teaching, and statements of episcopal conferences, Catholics are called to respect Muslims. An emphasis on peace and patience together with the encouragement to foster good relations with local Muslims is crucial, therefore, when preaching about Islam in any context.

Whether commenting on other faith communities or on the secular culture in which we are immersed, the homily is not a place for bitter invective, coarse rhetoric, or stereotypes and caricatures of other people's religious traditions or ethnic backgrounds. Prophetic challenge of false values is a legitimate and often necessary responsibility of preaching that draws its inspiration from Sacred Scripture. But the Eucharistic context of prayer and thanksgiving should encourage a tone of charity and respect in homilies even when using words of admonition or warning.

---

62   *Unitatis Redintegratio* (*Decree on Ecumenism*), no 15.
63   JPTSS, no. 87; *Nostra Aetate* (*Declaration on the Church's Relations with Non-Christian Religions*), no. 4.
64   See *Nostra Aetate*, no. 5.

IV. Interpreting the Scriptures and Preparing the Homily

Interpreting the Scriptures
in the Community of Faith

Preparing an effective homily necessarily entails interpretation of the Scriptures. In the context of preaching, such interpretation cannot be simply an intellectual exercise but must be a serious attempt to understand the Scriptures in the light of faith.

The homilist today has access to numerous resources for such a study of the Scriptures, including commentaries, articles, books, and websites from reliable Catholic sources. Several publishers also provide homily aids that are geared toward the Lectionary readings and provide both exegesis of the biblical passages and leads for preaching. Many priests and deacons use the Lectionary readings as an ongoing source for their prayer and meditation, merging homily preparation with their daily habit of prayer; for this, too, there have appeared several new resources that provide reflections on the Lectionary readings, drawing on both Patristic and contemporary sources.

The modern Church has benefited enormously from the historical-critical method of biblical interpretation, the stated purpose of which is to understand the intention of the particular human authors of the Scriptures as they addressed their own audiences and to reconstruct the historical and social context in which the biblical texts originated. Historical criticism reminds us that biblical religion, unlike mythic systems, is rooted in real events and persons and that God has deigned to reveal himself in the realities and particular circumstances of human history. This accords completely with the fundamental conviction of the Incarnation. Furthermore, the recovery of the original sense of the biblical books in their historical contexts enables the Church to set aside ungrounded and extravagant interpretations or unwarranted eisegesis—that is to say, reading into a text a meaning that is quite alien to it.[65]

As Pope Benedict XVI has observed, it is also important to augment use of the historical-critical method with other legitimate methodologies and, above all, with a perspective of faith. Probing a biblical text simply for its historical context or treating the biblical text from a purely scientific or empirical point of view is not sufficient when the purpose, as in liturgical preaching, is to open the meaning of the scriptural passage for Christian life today.[66] The Church has traditionally recognized that there are a variety of approaches to a faithful interpretation of the Scriptures summarized in the classical "fourfold senses" of Scripture.[67] The literal or historical sense remains fundamental, and other "spiritual" senses should be elaborated in relation to this fundamental sense, which probes the meaning intended by the biblical author. But one can also view the Scriptures from an "allegorical" perspective, linking biblical events or symbols based on the unity of the Scriptures, such as seeing in the crossing of the Red Sea a foreshadowing of the liberation from sin effected in Baptism. The "moral sense" focuses on how the events and teaching of Scripture guide us to act justly, while the "anagogical sense" reflects on biblical texts as signs or indicators of our eternal destiny. These approaches were a hallmark of Patristic preaching, which was characterized by a great love of Scriptures as a whole and a profound sense of communion with the Church. The Fathers did not have the resources of modern exegesis, but they were attuned to the various senses of the Scripture in their interpretation, and their preaching had a rich biblical resonance.[68]

Likewise, while appreciating the particular characteristics and theological perspective of an individual biblical book is helpful, Christian faith takes into account as well the entirety of the Bible as an inspired and sacred text. If we only focus on the diverse voices of the individual biblical books, we can lose a sense of the one voice of God as it speaks coherently and consistently through the whole of the Scriptures, especially as the entirety of Scriptures, from the truth of Christian faith, finds its ultimate coherence in the person

---

65 "The basic problem with fundamentalist interpretation of this kind is that, refusing to take into account the historical character of biblical revelation, it makes itself incapable of accepting the full truth of the incarnation itself" (*The Interpretation of the Bible in the Church*, Pontifical Biblical Commission [Rome, 1993]).

66 See *Verbum Domini*, nos. 35-41.

67 CCC, nos. 115-118; see also *The Interpretation of the Bible in the Church*, II, A, 2.

68 See *Verbum Domini*, no. 37.

and mission of Jesus Christ. Thus the Fathers of the Church delighted in typology—finding prefigurement of events in the life of Jesus or the Apostles in the great figures and experiences of Israel in the Old Testament. Homilists today, while respecting the integrity of the Old Testament as Scripture, can also artfully use the whole spectrum of the Bible to convey the message of the Gospel.[69]

The Magisterium of the Church, inspired by faith and the guidance of the Spirit, views theology and dogma not as distortions but as clarifying interpretive guides to the Bible, the reliable unfolding of the authentic meaning of the scriptural texts. Accordingly, the Church encourages exegetes and preachers to approach the Bible with a keen sense of the sacred text's essential unity as well as with an appreciation of how the *Logos*, Jesus Christ—articulated and developed theologically in the course of Sacred Tradition—provides the proper interpretive lens for the whole of Scripture.[70]

Preparation for Preaching the Homily

Fulfilled in Your Hearing provides practical advice about how best to prepare for the Sunday homily, advice that is still valid.[71] This text continues to serve as an important resource in many seminaries, permanent diaconate formation programs, and continuing education programs.

Good homiletic preaching begins and ends with an engagement with the word of God. Preparation begins several days before the Sunday liturgy with attentive reading of the assigned Scripture passages, listening to them in one's heart and mind and praying over them in silence. Next should come study of the text, perhaps consulting a good commentary or articles on these biblical texts, study that will trigger further reflection. The homilist may need to wrestle for a while with the challenging aspects of the biblical word, searching for ways it could connect to ordinary experience and how it might be proclaimed to the congregation the homilist serves. Then comes the process of drafting the homily in a thoughtful manner, finding the right words, moving examples, and apt metaphors that will bring home to the listener the beauty and truth of the Scripture—and then reviewing and revising the text of the homily until it is ready. Good homilists often practice their homily ahead of time, hearing how it sounds out loud and seeking to preach it with passion

---

69   See CCC, no. 130.
70   See CCC, nos. 128-129.
71   See *Fulfilled in Your Hearing*, 29-39.

and strength. Finally comes the moment of preaching itself. Normally the effective homilist will not be content to simply read a written text of his homily but will have so internalized what he wants to preach that the text or outline serves only as an aid to a direct proclamation of his message. Many priests and deacons will follow up their preaching by seeking out trusted friends or parish staff to ask how it came across and what could be done to make their homily even more effective.

The ministry of preaching, as the primary duty of the ordained priest, is worthy of this kind of hard work.[72] Over time, careful preparation and honest evaluation will ensure that the homilist will be more effective in the life-giving work of bringing God's word to the people.

Assisting Those Who Hear the Scriptures and the Homily

Just as the homilist must be immersed in study and reflection on the Scriptures to proclaim the Gospel faithfully, so too should members of the congregation who listen to the homily do what they can to receive properly and savor the biblical message. For this, there are numerous resources of various sorts on biblical study geared toward the lay reader, including increasing numbers of materials on the Internet and through social media. Catholics should be encouraged to prepare themselves beforehand for a fruitful encounter with God's word read and proclaimed in the context of the liturgy. This means not only thoughtful study of the historical background and context of the Bible but also the development of a habit of prayerful reflection upon the meaning of the biblical text as in the manner of *lectio divina*.

In addition to the study of and prayerful reflection on the biblical texts, there are other steps that the congregation can be encouraged to take. The liturgical celebration itself should properly accent the sacredness and importance of the biblical texts contained in the Lectionary by the beauty and artistry of the *Book of the Gospels*, the reverence shown it during the liturgy, the effective manner in which the Scriptures are proclaimed, the opportunity for

---

72   See *Presbyterorum Ordinis*, no. 4.

moments of silent meditation after they have been proclaimed, and also the proper use of Scripture in sacred song.[73]

Life-Long Growth in Preaching

Given the importance of the preaching ministry for the life and mission of the Church, it is not a surprise that becoming an effective homilist capable of bringing the message of the Scriptures into the life of the Christian community is a life-long and demanding process. Accordingly, the *Program for Priestly Formation* (PPF) as well as the *National Directory for the Formation, Ministry, and Life of Permanent Deacons in the United States* emphasize the importance of courses in Scripture along with other intellectual and spiritual formation in the Church's liturgy and dogma. Preparation for preaching also needs to include opportunities for supervised practice to develop the skills of the future preacher. Seminaries, schools of theology, permanent diaconate formation programs, and diocesan offices of continuing education for clergy are urged to offer in-service courses and workshops for priests and deacons in order to review the quality and manner of their preaching and to find ways to continue to develop their ministry of the word.[74]

---

73 See *Verbum Domini*, no. 66; *Sacrosanctum Concilium*, no. 30; GIRM, no. 56.
74 See *Basic Plan for the Ongoing Formation of Priests* (USCCB, 2001).

CONCLUSION

Mary as Hearer and Bearer of the Word

Mary, the Mother of God and Mother of the Word Incarnate, can serve as an example for those who preach the Sunday homily. Mary is "the one in whom the interplay between the word of God and faith was brought to perfection."[75] When she heard the word, she listened intently and responded with an unhesitating "yes." This is why Church Fathers, such as St. Ephrem and St. Augustine, could say that Mary conceived the word in her heart before conceiving the Word in her womb. Mary surveyed the great events surrounding the Birth of her Son, and she treasured them in her heart. Her response revealed a profound contemplative spirit that strove to understand God's will for her and the destiny of her Son (Lk 2:19, 51). At the wedding feast of Cana, Mary turned to the table servants and quietly instructed them: "Do whatever he tells you," revealing thereby her intense focus on Jesus and her docility to his word (Jn 2:1-12). In her *Magnificat*, the Mother of Jesus spoke as her Son would, fearlessly proclaiming the prophetic word (Lk 1:46-55). For all of these reasons, Pope Benedict XVI says, "Mary is the image of the Church in attentive hearing of the word of God, which took flesh in her."[76]

And so we conclude by appealing to you, our dearest brothers, who share with us this sacred responsibility of hearing and proclaiming the word. As we all know, our beloved Church today faces many challenges and great opportunities. Some of the challenges can seem overwhelming and beyond our power to address. Many priests and deacons feel overburdened. Yet we are the Church of Jesus Christ, and we believe that the Spirit that first animated those confused and fearful disciples in the Upper Room is still with us. There may be some things we can do little about on our own and have to leave in the merciful and loving hands of the Risen Christ. But our ministry of preaching is something all of us can address and improve. Each of us, drawing strength from our people and in communion with the whole Church, can pray the Scriptures more intensely, can prepare our homilies more intently,

---

75   *Verbum Domini*, no. 27.
76   *Verbum Domini*, no. 27.

and can give all our mind and heart to bringing the Good News of Jesus Christ to our people gathered before us at the Eucharist. In union with the bishops of the whole Church, the Holy Father has encouraged us to make this a new era of proclaiming the Gospel to our Catholic people and indeed to the whole world.

May we who are ordained to preach the Sunday homily, like Mary who brought the Incarnate Word into the world, conform our lives to her Son and proclaim effectively the word of salvation to all.